Viola Time Sprinters

a third book of pieces for viola

Kathy and David Blackwell

Welcome to *Viola Time Sprinters*. You'll find:

- pieces using the finger pattern 01–2–34, plus low 2nd fingers and high 3rd fingers
- 2nd and 3rd position pieces
- a range of bowing techniques, including spiccato, hooked bowing, and string crossing
- original pieces in different styles plus well-known pieces
- pieces using modes, the chromatic and blues scales, and dominant 7ths
- duets with parts of equal difficulty
- CD of performances and backings, with drumkit and bass added for the jazz and rock numbers
- piano and viola accompaniments available separately.

Pieces with piano accompaniment are presented in two formats on the CD: firstly, a complete performance, then the accompaniment only, which you can play along to. There is a count-in when the viola and piano parts start together.

 This symbol is placed alongside all the pieces that appear on the accompanying CD. When there are two numbers given in the symbol, the top number indicates the complete performance, and the bottom number the accompaniment alone.

In all duet pieces, the top part is assigned to the right-hand channel and the lower part to the left-hand channel. You can choose to play along with either part by muting the appropriate channel.

MUSIC DEPARTMENT

OXFORD
UNIVERSITY PRESS

OXFORD

UNIVERSITY PRESS

Great Clarendon Street, Oxford OX2 6DP, England

Oxford University Press is a department of the University of Oxford.
It furthers the University's aim of excellence in research, scholarship,
and education by publishing worldwide

Music and text origination by
Barnes Music Engraving Ltd., East Sussex

Printed in Great Britain on acid-free paper by
Halstan & Co. Ltd., Amersham, Bucks.

Contents

1. Ready to rock

KB & DB

Determined

f

2. Clear skies

KB & DB

Relaxed

mp

cresc.

rit.

mp

p

3. Ode to joy

(from Symphony No. 9)

Ludwig van Beethoven (1770–1827)

Joyfully

Also try this in 3rd position using the fingering given.

4. Song from the show

KB & DB

5. Starry night

KB & DB

6. Paris café

KB & DB

7. Gaudete!

Medieval carol

8. Jacob's dance

KB & DB

Rhythmic

9. Sprint finish

KB & DB

Fast

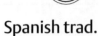

10. Bolero

Spanish trad.

This piece can be played as a solo or duet with piano, or as an unaccompanied viola duet.

11. **William Tell**

G. A. Rossini (1792–1868)

Warm up

staccato

Repeat an octave higher.

12. Country gardens

English Morris Dance tune

5

9

13

17

21

25

29

Warm up

etc.

Try a C major scale/arpeggio with hooked bowing.

15. Full circle

KB & DB

Gently

16. Thirsty work

KB & DB

Variation: the chorus and verse 1 can be played in semiquavers with spiccato bowing, as demonstrated in the final chorus on the CD.

Warm ups

Repeat on the D and A strings.

17. Farewell to Skye

KB & DB

18. Lady Katherine's pavane

KB & DB

The pavane was a slow, stately court dance popular in the 16th and 17th centuries.

19. *Dance of the Sugar Plum Fairy*

(from the *Nutcracker* ballet)

P. I. Tchaikovsky (1840–93)

20. *Allegro in D*

G. P. Telemann (1681–1767)

Try starting this piece with either a down or an up bow.

21. *Still reeling*

(based on *Blair Atholl*, trad. Scottish reel)

arr. KB & DB

Add your own dynamics to this reel.

A second player could add a drone accompaniment using these two chords; how about a drum/bodran rhythm too?

22. Mexican fiesta

KB & DB

Use these words to help with the rhythm:

Tro - pi - cal heat-wave in   Mex - i - co

23. Show stopper

KB & DB

24. Spy movie

KB & DB

Creepy

25. Largo

(from the *New World* Symphony)

Antonín Dvořák (1841–1904)

27. *Hungarian folk dance*

KB & DB

Warm ups

Try these two warm ups in the Lydian mode.

28. *Wild West*

KB & DB

Warm up

Use this warm up to practise changing quickly from 1st to 3rd position.

29. *Midnight song*

KB & DB

Peaceful

mp legato espress.

dim.

mf

mf

cresc.

mp

rall.

dim.

p

Warm up

Practise legato shifts from 1st to 3rd position with this warm up.

Also try on the G and A strings.

30. Wade in the water

Spiritual

Warm ups

Sing and play this warm up a few times to get the feel of the syncopated rhythm.

Wade_____ in the wa - ter,___

Play the blues scale on G.

Play this rhythm on each note of the blues scale on G.

31. Dominant gene

KB & DB

With attitude

f marcato

f marcato

5

9

13

ff

ff

sub. p

sub. p

16

molto rall.

cresc.

f

ff

cresc.

f

ff

32. Chromatic cats

KB & DB

33. Show off!

KB & DB

Warm ups

Play an F major scale in 2nd position like this:

Lit - tle   lamb,   oh   lit - tle   lamb,   oh

etc.

35. *Habanera*
(from *Carmen*)

Georges Bizet (1838–75)

Allegretto quasi Andantino

Warm up

To get the feel of the triplet rhythm, try playing a chromatic scale on G with this pattern:

etc.

Have a si - es - ta, have a si - es - ta, have a si - es - ta,

Round up

Play these rounds or canons in 2 or more parts, entering at *.

36. Alleluia

William Boyce (1711–79)

37. Jubilate Deo

W. A. Mozart (1756–91)

38. Round Trinidad Bay

KB & DB